PRAYER

PRAYER

Encounter with the Living God

Metropolitan Hilarion (Alfeyev)
of Volokolamsk

Translated from the Russian by
Hierodeacon Samuel

ST VLADIMIR'S SEMINARY PRESS
YONKERS, NY
2015

Library of Congress Cataloging-in-Publication Data

Ilarion, Metropolitan of Volokolamsk, 1966– author.
  [O molitve. English]
  Prayer : encounter with the living God / By Metropolitan Hilarion
  (Alfeyev) of Volokolamsk; translated from the Russian by Hierodeacon
  Samuel
     pages cm
  In English; translated from Russian.
  ISBN 978-0-88141-528-5 (pbk.)—ISBN 978-0-88141-529-2 (electronic)
  1.   Prayer—Orthodox Eastern Church. 2.   Spiritual life—Orthodox
  Eastern Church. I.   Title.
  BX382.I482 2015
  248.3'2—DC23

                                                            2015025651

*The following thirty-two part series on prayer was transcribed and
translated from television episodes presented on Russian television in
the spring of 1999 by Igumen (now Metropolitan) Hilarion (Alfeyev)
with the blessing of His Holiness, the late Patriarch Alexei II of
Moscow and All Russia.*

ST VLADIMIR'S SEMINARY PRESS
575 Scarsdale Road, Yonkers, NY 10707
www.svspress.com • 1-800-204-2665

ISBN 978-0-88141-528-5

PRINTED IN THE UNITED STATES OF AMERICA

Contents

1

Prayer as Encounter

Prayer is an encounter with the Living God. Christianity gives man direct access to God, who listens to man, helps him, and loves him. This is the fundamental difference between Christianity and, for example, Buddhism, in which during meditation the one praying deals with a certain impersonal super-being, in which he is immersed and in which he is dissolved, but he does not feel God as a living Person. In Christian prayer, man feels the presence of the Living God.

The God who became man is revealed to us in Christianity. When we stand before an icon of Jesus Christ, we contemplate the incarnate God. We know that it is impossible to represent, depict, or portray

God on an icon or picture. But it is possible to depict the God who became man, because he revealed himself to people. Through Jesus Christ as man we uncover God for ourselves. This uncovering takes place in prayer, in conversion to Christ.

Through prayer we know that God participates in everything that takes place in our lives. Therefore, conversation with God should not take place in the background of our lives, but should be its main content. There are many barriers between man and God that can be overcome only with the help of prayer.

It is often asked: why do we need to pray, to ask God for something, if God already knows what we need? This is how I would reply. We do not pray in order to beg for something from God. Yes, in some cases we do ask him for specific help in various everyday circumstances. But this should not be the main content of prayer.

God cannot only be an "intermediate agent" in our earthly affairs. The main content of prayer should always be standing before God, an encounter with him. We need to pray in order to be with God, to come into contact with God, to feel God's presence.

However, an encounter with God does not always take place in prayer. After all, even when meeting with a person we are not always able to overcome the barriers that divide us and to descend into the depths; often our communication with people is confined to the surface level. So it is in prayer, too. Sometimes we feel that between God and us there is a kind of blank wall, that God does not hear us. But we should understand that God did not place this barrier there: we ourselves have erected it through our sins. In the words of one Western medieval theologian, God is always next to us, but we are often far from him; God always hears us, but we do not hear him; God is always within us, but we are on the outside; God is at home in us, but we are strangers to him.

Let us remember this when we are preparing for prayer. Let us remember that every time we stand in prayer we are coming into contact with the Living God.

2

Prayer as Dialogue

Prayer is a dialogue. It includes not only our own turning towards God, but also the response of God himself. As in every dialogue, in prayer it is important not only to speak out and express ourself, but also to listen to the response. God's response does not always come directly in the minutes of prayer; sometimes it happens somewhat later. It can happen, for example, that we ask God for immediate help, but it only comes after several hours or days. But we understand that it took place because we asked God for help in prayer.

Through prayer we can learn a great deal about God. When praying, it is very important to be prepared for what God reveals to us; but he can prove to be other than we had imagined him. Often we make the mistake of approaching God with our own ideas about him, and these ideas can obscure from us the real image of the Living God, which God himself can reveal to us. Often people create in their own minds a kind of idol and then pray to this idol. This dead, artificially created idol becomes an obstacle or barrier between the Living God and us people. "Make yourself a false image of God and try praying to him. Make yourself an image of an unmerciful and cruel Judge, and try praying to him with confidence and love," remarked Metropolitan Anthony of Sourozh. Thus, we should be ready for God to reveal himself as different than we had imagined him. Therefore, approaching prayer, you must abandon all images that our human imagination and fantasy produce.

God's response can take place in different ways, but prayer is never unrequited. If we do not hear a response, it means that something is not right in us ourselves; it means that we have not yet sufficiently tuned ourselves to the right way for encountering God.

There is an instrument called a tuning fork, used for tuning pianos; this device gives the clear sound of an "A." The strings of the piano must be strung in such a way that the sound they produce is in strict accordance with the sound of the tuning fork. As long as the "A" string is not sufficiently taut, no matter how many times you hit the keys, the tuning fork will remain silent. But the moment the string reaches the necessary degree of tension, the tuning fork—a lifeless piece of metal—will suddenly begin to sound. Having adjusted the one "A" string, the master can then configure this "A" in the other octaves (in a piano each key strikes several strings, creating a special "surround" sound). Then he can set the "B," "C," and so forth, one octave after another, until finally the entire instrument will be configured in accordance with the tuning fork.

So it must be with us in prayer. We should tune in to God, adjusting our entire life—all the strings of our soul—to him. When we adjust our life to God; when we learn to fulfill his commandments; when the Gospel becomes our moral and spiritual law; and when we learn to live in accordance with God's commandments, then we begin to feel how the soul responds to the presence of God in prayer, just as a tuning fork responds to an perfectly stretched string.

3

When Should We Pray?

When and how long should you pray? The Apostle Paul writes: "Pray without ceasing" (1 Thess 5.17). St Gregory the Theologian writes: "One needs to remember God more often than one breathes." Ideally, the Christian's entire life should be imbued with prayer.

Many troubles, sorrows, and tribulations come about because people forget about God. There are criminals who are believers, but at the moment they commit their crimes they did not think about God. It is hard to imagine someone who would commit a murder or theft while thinking about the all-seeing God, from whom no evil is hidden. And man commits all sin precisely at those times that he does not remember God.

The majority of people are not able to pray during the course of the day, for this reason you need to find a time, even if a short one, when you can remember God.

In the morning you wake up with thoughts about what needs to be done that day. Before you begin work and become immersed in the inevitable bustle, dedicate at least a few minutes to God. Stand before God and say: "Lord, thou hast given me this day; help me to spend it without sin, without blemish; keep me from all evil and misfortune." And invoke God's blessing on the day that is beginning.

Throughout the course of the entire day, strive to remember God more frequently. If you do not feel well, turn to him with prayer: "Lord, I am not well; help me." If you feel well, say to God: "Lord, glory to Thee; I thank Thee for this joy." If you are worried about someone, tell God: "Lord, I am worried for him; I am concerned about him; help him." And so forth throughout the course of the day: whatever happens to you, put it into prayer.

When the day has come to an end and you are ready for bed, remember the past day, thank God for all good things that have taken place, and offer repentance for all those unworthy deeds and sins that you have committed during the day. Ask for God's help and blessing for the coming night. If you learn to pray like this over the course of every day, you will soon notice how much sounder your life will become.

People often justify their reluctance to pray by the fact that they are too busy and are overloaded with things to do. Yes, many of us live in a sort of rhythm unlike that of people of antiquity. Sometimes we have to do a great number of things over the course of the day. But in life there are always certain pauses. For example, we might stand at the bus stop for three to five minutes; if we take the train, for twenty or thirty minutes. We dial a number and get a busy signal— another few minutes. Let us at least use these pauses for prayer; let it at least not be wasted time.

4

Short Prayers

People often ask: how should we pray, in what words, and in what language? Some even say: "I do not pray because I do not know how; I do not know any prayers." You do not need any specialized skill for prayer. You can simply talk with God. Many Orthodox Churches across the world use a special language in the divine services, such as Church Slavonic or Koine Greek. But in private prayer, when we are alone with God, there is no need for any special language. We can pray to God in the language we use when speaking with people, when thinking.

Prayer should be very simple. St Isaac the Syrian said: "The whole fabric of your prayer should be succinct.

One word saved the publican, and one word made the thief on the cross heir to the heavenly kingdom."

Let us recall the parable of the Publican and the Pharisee: "Two men went up into the temple to pray: the one a Pharisee, and the other a publican. The Pharisee stood and prayed thus with himself: 'God, I thank thee, that I am not as other men, extortioners, unjust, adulterers, or even as this publican. I fast twice a week, I give tithes of all that I possess.' And the publican, standing afar off, would not even lift up his eyes to heaven, but beat his breast, saying, 'God, be merciful to me a sinner'" (Lk 18.10-13). And this short prayer saved him. Let us also remember the thief who was crucified with Jesus and who said to him: Lord, remember me when thou comest into thy kingdom (Lk 23.42). This alone was enough for him to enter Paradise.

Prayer can be extremely brief. If you are just starting out on your path of prayer, begin with very short prayers, such as can allow you to focus. God does not need words; he needs men's hearts. Words are secondary; of paramount importance are the feeling and disposition with which we approach God. To approach God without a feeling of reverence or with distraction—when during prayer our mind wanders—is much more dangerous than saying the wrong words in prayer. Distracted prayer has neither meaning nor value. A simple law is at work: if the words of prayer do not reach our heart, they will not reach God. As it is sometimes put, such prayer does not reach above the ceiling of the room in which we are praying, and it should reach the heavens. Therefore it is very important that each word of prayer should be felt deeply by us. If you are incapable of focusing on the long prayers contained in the prayer books of the Orthodox Church, try your hand at shorter prayers: "Lord, have mercy," "Lord, save," "Lord, help me," "God, have mercy on me, the sinner."

One ascetic struggler said that if we could, with the full force of our feelings—with all our heart and soul—just say the prayer "Lord, have mercy," then that would be enough for salvation. But the problem is that, as a rule, we cannot say this with all our heart; we cannot say this with all our whole life. Therefore, in order to be heard by God, we tend to use many words.

Let us remember that God longs for our hearts, not for our words. If we turn to him with our whole hearts, then we will certainly get a response.

5

Prayer and Life

Prayer involves not only joy and attainments, which take place because of it, but also painstaking daily labor. Sometimes prayer brings enormous joy, refreshing man and giving him new strength and opportunities. But it very often happens that you are not disposed towards prayer, that you do not want to pray. Because of this, prayer should not depend upon our mood. Prayer is labor. St Silouan the Athonite said, "To pray is to shed blood." As with every labor, it requires great effort, sometimes enormous effort, to force yourself to pray even when you do not want to. And such an effort will be repaid one hundredfold.

But why do we sometimes not want to pray? I think that the main reason for this is the fact that our life does not correspond to prayer, is not configured for it. In childhood, when I was in music school, I had an excellent violin teacher: his lessons were very interesting, but sometimes very difficult—but it depended not on his mood, but rather on how well or poorly I had prepared for the lesson. If I had practiced a great deal, learned a given piece and come to class fully prepared, then the lesson went by at one go, and both the teacher and I were pleased. But if I put it off all week and came unprepared, then the teacher would be upset and it was sickening to me that the lesson did not go as I had hoped.

It is exactly the same with prayer. If our life is not a preparation for prayer, then it can be very difficult for us to pray. Prayer is the gauge of our spiritual life, a kind of litmus test. We need to construct our life in such a way that it conforms to prayer. When reciting the prayer "Our Father," we say: "Lord, thy will be done," which means that we should always be ready to fulfill God's will, even if this will contradicts our human will. When we say to God: "And forgive us our trespasses [or *debts*], as we forgive our trespasses [or *debtors*]," we thereby commit ourselves to pardoning people and forgiving their debts, because if we do not forgive our debtors, then, by the logic of this prayer, God will not forgive us our debts.

Thus, the one must correspond to the other: life to prayer, and prayer to life. Without this correspondence we will not succeed either in life or in prayer.

Let us not hesitate if we find it difficult to pray. This means that God is presenting us with new challenges, which we should resolve both in prayer and in life. If we learn to live in accordance with the Gospel, then we will learn to pray in accordance with the Gospel. Then our life will become complete, spiritual, and truly Christian.

6

Orthodox Prayer Books

You can pray in different ways, in your own words, for example. Such prayer should be a constant companion. Morning and evening, day and night, you can turn to God with simple words coming from the depths of your heart.

But there are also prayers that were compiled by the saints in antiquity, which need to be read in order to learn how to pray. These prayers are contained in the "Orthodox Prayer Book." There you will find prayers for the morning and evening, for repentance and thanksgiving, along with various canons, akathists, and much else. When you purchase an "Orthodox Prayer Book," do not be alarmed that there are so many prayers. You do not have to read all of them.

If the morning prayers are read quickly, this takes about twenty minutes. But if you read them thoughtfully and carefully, responding in your heart to each word, then reading them can take a whole hour. Therefore, if you do not have time, do not try to read all the morning prayers; it is better to read one or two, but in such a way that every word reaches your heart.

Before the section with the "Morning Prayers," we read: "Having risen from sleep, before any other action, stand reverently, considering thyself to be in the presence of the All-seeing God, and, having made the sign of the Cross, say: 'In the Name of the Father, and of the Son, and of the Holy Spirit. Amen.' Then pause a moment, until all thy senses are calmed and thy thoughts forsake all things earthly." This pause, this "moment of silence," before beginning to pray is very important. Prayer should grow out of the quietness of our hearts. People who daily "read through" the morning and evening prayers constantly have the temptations of reading the "rule" as quickly as possible in order to get on with the business of the day. Often, with such reading, the most important thing—the content of the prayers—is missed.

In the Prayer Book there are many petitions addressed to God that are repeated many times. For example, you can come across the recommendation to repeat "Lord, have mercy" twelve or forty times. Some people see this as some kind of formality and read this prayer as quickly as possible. By the way, in Greek "Lord, have mercy" is "Kyrie, eleison." In Russian there is the verb *kurolesit'* [to play tricks], which came from the fact that readers on the kliros often quickly or repeatedly read "Kyrie, eleison"—that is, they were not praying, but were playing. Thus, in prayer you do not need to play tricks [*kurolesit'*]. No matter how many times this prayer is read, it should be spoken with care, reverence, and love, with full delivery.

You do not need to try to read through all the prayers. It is better to dedicate twenty minutes to the single prayer "Our Father," repeating it several times, pondering every word. It is not easy for someone who is not accustomed to prayer immediately to read through a large number of prayers—and this is not something to which one should aspire. It is important to become imbued with the spirit that is breathed by the prayers of the Church Fathers. This is the main benefit to be derived from the prayers contained in the "Orthodox Prayer Book."

7

Prayer Rules

What is a prayer rule? These are prayers that you read regularly, daily. Everyone has a different prayer rule. For one person, the morning or evening prayers take up several hours, while for another they take a few minutes. Everything depends on your spiritual disposition, on the degree of your rootedness in prayer, and on how much time you have.

It is very important that to keep a prayer rule, even a very short one, so that you would be regular and constant in prayer. But the rule should not turn into a formality. The experience of many believers shows that, by constantly reading through the same prayers, their words can become colorless: they lose their freshness, and one who has become used to them can no longer focus on them. This danger needs to be avoided at all costs.

I remember that when I received the monastic tonsure (I was then twenty years old), I turned for advice to an experienced spiritual father, asking him what sort of prayer rule I should have. He said: "You should daily read through the morning and evening prayers, three canons, and one akathist. Whatever happens, even if you are very tired, you are obliged to read them. And even if you read through them quickly and inattentively, that is not important. The main thing is that the rule be read through." I tried. It did not take. The daily reading of the same prayers led to these texts quickly becoming boring. Besides, I spent many hours daily in church at services that spiritually nourished, fed, and inspired me. But reading through these three canons and an akathist turned into some unnecessary kind of "appendage." I began to seek out different advice, more suitable to me. And I found it in the works of St Theophan the Recluse, that remarkable nineteenth-century ascetic struggler. He advised calculating your prayer rule not from the number of prayers, but from the time that we are prepared to dedicate to God. For example, we can take as a rule to pray in the morning and evening for half an hour, but these half hours should be wholly given over to God. And it is less important whether we read all the prayers or only one during these minutes, or if we dedicate an evening entirely to reading the Psalter, the Gospel, or to praying in our own words. The most important thing is to be focused on God, that our attention not run away, and that every word reach our heart. This advice worked for me. However, I do not exclude that for others the advice I obtained from my spiritual father might be more appropriate. Here a great deal depends on personality.

It seems to me that, for someone living in the world, not only fifteen but even five minutes of morning and evening prayer can be enough to be a true Christian— as long, of course, as they are said with attention and feeling. It is important only that your thoughts always correspond to the words, that the heart respond to the words of the prayers, that your whole life correspond to prayer.

Following the advice of St Theophan the Recluse, try to set aside some time for prayer in the course of the day and for the fulfillment of a daily prayer rule. And you will see that this will quickly bear fruit.

8

The Danger of Habituation

Every believer faces the danger of becoming habituated to the words of prayer and of becoming distracted during prayer. In order to avoid this, you must do constant battle with yourself, or, as the Holy Fathers put it, to "guard your mind" and learn "to enclose your mind in the words of prayer."

But how to achieve this? First of all, you should not allow yourself to pronounce words when your mind and heart do not respond to them. If you begin to read a prayer, but in the middle your attention strays, go back to the place where your attention strayed and repeat the prayer. If necessary, repeat it three, five, or ten times—but get to the point that your whole being responds to it.

Once in church a lady appealed to me: "Batiushka, I have read prayers for many years: both the morning and the evening prayers, but the more I read them, the less I like them, and the less I feel myself believing in God. I am so tired of the words of these prayers that I no longer respond to them."

I said to her: "Do not read the morning or evening prayers."

She was astonished: "What do you mean?"

I repeated: "Put them away; do not read them. If your heart does not respond to them, you need to find another means of prayer. How much time do your morning prayers take?"

"Twenty minutes."

"Are you ready to dedicate twenty minutes every morning to God?"

"I'm ready."

"Then take one morning prayer—your choice—and read it over the course of twenty minutes. Read one phrase, be silent, and think about what it means.

Then read another phrase, be silent, and think about its content. Repeat it again, thinking about whether it corresponds to your life, whether you are ready to live in such a way that this prayer would become real in your life. You read: 'Lord, deprive me not of thy heavenly goods.' What does that mean? Or: 'Lord, deliver me from eternal torments.' What is the danger of these eternal torments? Do we actually fear them? Do we really hope to be delivered from them?" The woman began to pray in this way, and soon her prayer began to revive.

You must learn to pray. You need to work on yourself; you cannot allow yourself to stand before icons and utter empty words.

The quality of prayer also manifests itself by what precedes it and by what follows it. It is impossible to focus on prayer when you are angry or, for example, if before beginning to pray you have argued with some-body or shouted at someone. This means that in the time preceding prayer we should prepare ourselves for it inwardly, freeing ourselves from whatever inter-feres with our prayer, and creating within ourselves a prayerful disposition. Then it will be easier for us to pray. And, of course, after prayer you should not immediately give yourself over to bustle. Having finished praying, give yourself some time to hear God's response, so that something might sound in you in response to God's presence.

Prayer is valuable only when we feel that, thanks to it, something changes in us, that we begin to live differently. Prayer can bear fruit, and these fruits should be felt.

9

The Disposition of the Body at Prayer

In the prayer practice of the early Church, various poses, gestures, and bodily positions were used. People prayed standing, or kneeling in the so-called position of the Prophet Elijah—that is, standing on your knees with your head bowed to the ground—or lying on the floor with outstretched hands, or standing with upraised hands. Prostrations were employed in prayer: both full prostrations and bows from the waist, as well as the sign of the cross. Of all the various traditional positions of the body in prayer, only a few have remained in contemporary practice. These are above all prayer standing and prayer kneeling, accompanied by the sign of the cross and bows.

Why is it important that the body participate in prayer? Why can't you simply pray in spirit while lying in bed or sitting on an armchair? In principle, you can pray either lying down or sitting: in special circumstances, such as in illness or when travelling, this is done. But under normal circumstances it is necessary while praying to make use of the dispositions of the body that have been preserved in the tradition of the Orthodox Church. The fact is that body and spirit are inextricably linked in man, and the spirit cannot act completely autonomously from the body. It was no accident that the ancient Fathers said: "If the body does not labor in prayer, then prayer will remain fruitless."

Go into an Orthodox church during Great Lent and you will see how from time to time all the parishioners fall on their knees, then get up, then again fall and get up. And such goes on for the duration of the service. You will feel that there is a special intensity to this service, that people are not simply praying, but are laboring in prayer, bearing the heroic feat of prayer. Then go into a Protestant church. During the course of the entire service, the worshippers are sitting: prayers are read and spiritual songs are sung, but people remain sitting, neither crossing themselves nor bowing, while at the end of the service they all get up and leave. Compare these two means of prayer in church—Orthodox and Protestant—in terms of intensity of prayer. People are praying to one and the same God, but they are praying differently. And this difference is largely determined by the physical dispositions of those praying.

Prostrations help prayer a great deal. Those of you who are able in your morning or evening prayer rule do to at least a few bows and prostrations will undoubtedly feel how helpful this is in spiritual terms. The body becomes more collected, and when the body is collected, composure of mind and attention comes much more naturally.

During prayer we should from time to time make the sign of the cross, especially when we say "In the Name of the Father, and of the Son, and of the Holy Spirit," as well as when we pronounce the name of the Savior. This is necessary because the cross is the weapon of our salvation. When we place the sign of the cross on ourselves, God's power becomes tangibly present in us.

10

Prayer before Icons

In prayer the outward should not replace the inward. The outward should contribute to the inward, but it can also hinder it. The traditional disposition of the body at prayer undoubtedly contributes to a prayerful state, but can in no way serve as a substitute for the main content of prayer.

You should not forget that certain dispositions of the body are not accessible to everyone. For example, many older people are simply incapable of making full prostrations. There are many people who cannot stand for long. I have heard from older people: "I do not go to services at church because I cannot stand," or "I do not pray to God, because my legs hurt." God does not need our legs, but our hearts. If you cannot pray standing up, then pray sitting down; if you cannot pray sitting down, then pray laying down. As one ascetic struggler put it: "better to sit thinking about God, than to stand thinking about your legs."

Auxiliary means are important, but they should not take the place of content. One of the most important auxiliary means for prayer is the icon. Orthodox Christians, as a rule, pray before icons of the Savior, the Mother of God, the saints, and before depictions of the Holy Cross. But Protestants pray without icons. You can see here the difference between Protestant and Orthodox prayer. In the Orthodox tradition, prayer is more concrete. Contemplating the icon of Christ, we look as if through a window opening up another world to us; behind this icon stands the One to whom we are praying.

But it is very important that the icon not replace the object of prayer, so that we would not address ourselves in prayer to the icon or try to imagine the person depicted on the icon. The icon is only a reminder, only a kind of symbol of the reality that is behind it. As the Church Fathers say, "the honor rendered to the image passes over to the prototype." When we approach an icon of the Savior or the Mother of God and venerate it—that is, kiss it—we are thereby expressing our love for the Savior or the Mother of God.

Icons should not be turned into idols. Nor should there be the illusion that God is as he is depicted on icons. There exists, for example, an icon of the Holy Trinity called the "New Testament Trinity": it is unca-nonical—that is, it does not correspond to the rules of the Church—but you can see it in certain churches. On this icon God the Father is depicted as a grey-haired old man, Jesus Christ as a young man, and the Holy Spirit in the form of a dove. By no means should we be tempted to imagine that the Holy Trinity looks like this. The Holy Trinity is God, who cannot be rep-resented by the human imagination. And, turning to God the Holy Trinity in prayer, we should renounce every kind of fantasy. Our imagination should be free from images; the mind should be crystal clear; and the heart should be ready to accommodate the Living God.

My car once fell off a precipice, rolling over several times. Nothing was left of it, but the driver and I were safe and sound. This took place early in the morn-ing, around five. When I returned to the church in which I served that same evening, I encountered a few parishioners who had awoken at half past four in the morning, sensing danger, and who had begun to pray for me.

Their first question was: "Batiushka, what happened to you?" I think that it was through their prayers that both the driver and I were saved from disaster.

We should pray for our neighbors not because God does not know how to save them, but because he wants us to participate in one another's salvation. Of course, he himself knows what everyone needs—both what we need, and what our neighbors need. When we pray for our neighbors, this does not at all mean that we want to be more merciful than God. But it does mean that we want to participate in their salvation. In prayer, we should not forget the people life has brought to us, nor should we forget their prayers for us. Each of us, when we go to sleep at night, can say to God: "Lord, through the prayers of all those who love me, save me!"

Let us remember the living connection between our neighbors and us, and let us always remember one another in prayer.

11

Prayer for Our Neighbors

We should pray not only for ourselves, but also for our neighbors. Every morning and every evening, as well as when we are in church, we should remember our relatives, family, friends, enemies, and offer prayer to God for them all. This is very important, because people are bound together by indissoluble bonds and often the prayer of one person for another saves the other from great danger.

In the Life of St Gregory the Theologian there is the following incident. When he was still a young man and unbaptized, he crossed the Mediterranean by ship. A heavy storm suddenly began, which lasted for many days, and no one had any hope of rescue; the ship was almost flooded. Gregory prayed to God and, during his prayer, saw his mother, who was then on the shore but who, as it later turned out, felt the danger and fervently prayed for her son. The ship, contrary to all expectations, reached the shore safely. Gregory always remembered that his deliverance came about as a result of his mother's prayers.

Someone might say: "Well, that's just another story from the lives of the ancient saints. Why don't similar things happen today?" I can assure you that they do happen today. I know many people who were saved from death or great danger by the prayers of their loved ones. And in my own life there have been many cases when I was saved from danger by the prayers of my mother or other people, such as my parishioners.

I was once in a car accident and one might say that I stayed alive miraculously, because the car fell off a precipice and rolled over several times. Nothing remained of the car, but the driver and I were left safe and sound. This took place early in the morning, around five. When I returned to the church in which I was serving that same evening, I found several parishioners who had awakened at half past four in the morning and, sensing danger, had begun to pray for me. Their first question was: "Batiushka, what happened to you?" I think that it was by their prayers that the driver and I were saved from disaster.

We should pray for our neighbors not because God does not know how to save them, but because he wants us to participate in one another's salvation. Of course, he himself knows what everyone needs: both what we need, and what our neighbors need. When we pray for our neighbors, it does not at all mean that we want to be more merciful than God. What it does mean is that we want to participate in their salvation. And in prayer we should not forget about the people with whom life has brought us together, and that they also pray for us. Each of us, laying down to sleep, should say to God: "Lord, through the prayers of all those who love me, save me!"

Let us remember the living connection between our neighbors and us, and let us always remember one another in prayer.

12

Prayer for the Departed

We should pray not only for our neighbors who are alive, but also for those who have departed to the other world.

Prayer for the departed is necessary first of all because, when someone who is close to us departs, we have a natural feeling of loss, from which we suffer deeply. But that person continues to live: only he lives in another dimension, because he has left for the other world. So that our connection with him who has departed might not be broken, we should pray for him. Then we will feel his presence, feel that he has not left us, and that our living connection with him has been preserved.

But the other person, of course, also needs prayer for the departed, because when someone dies they pass into another world, where they meet God to answer for everything they did in their earthly life, good and bad. It is very important that such a person be accompanied on his way by the prayers of his loved ones, of those who have remained here on earth, who keep his memory. We, who remain on earth, can ask God that he lighten this person's lot. And the Church believes that the departed's posthumous lot is lightened by the prayers of those who pray for him here on earth.

The hero of Dostoevsky's novel *The Brothers Karamazov*, the Elder Zosima (whose prototype was St Tikhon of Zadonsk) says this about prayer for the departed: "Remember also: every day and whenever you can, repeat within yourself: 'Lord, have mercy upon all who come before you today.' For every hour and every moment thousands of people leave their life on this earth, and their souls come before the Lord—and so many of them part with the earth in isolation, unknown to anyone, in sadness and sorrow that no one will mourn for them, or even know whether they had lived or not. And so, perhaps from the other end of the earth, your prayer for his repose will rise to the Lord, though you did not known him at all, nor he you. How moving it is for his soul, coming in fear before the Lord, to feel at that moment that someone is praying for him, too, that there is still a human being on earth who loves him. And God, too, will look upon you both with more mercy, for if even you so pitied him, how much more will he who is infinitely more merciful and loving than you are. And he will forgive him for your sake."

13

Prayer for Our Enemies

The necessity of praying for our enemies stems from the very essence of the moral teaching of Jesus Christ.

In the pre-Christian era there was a rule: You shall love your neighbor and hate your enemy (Mt 5.43). The majority of people continue to live in accordance with this rule. It is natural for us to love our neighbors, those who do us good, and to treat with hostility and even hatred those who present us with evil. But Christ says that our attitude should be completely different: "Love your enemies and pray for those who persecute you" (Mt 5:44).

Christ himself, during his earthly life, repeatedly set an example both of love for enemies and of prayer for them. When the soldiers nailed the Lord to the Cross, he experienced frightful torments and incredible pain, but he prayed: "Father, forgive them; for they know not what they do" (Lk 23.34). At that moment he thought not about himself, not about the fact that these soldiers were causing him pain, but rather about their salvation; for, by committing evil, they were first of all harming themselves.

We should remember that people who do us evil or treat us with hostility are not bad in themselves. What is bad is the sin with which they are infected. We must hate sin, but not its bearer: man. As St John Chrysostom put it: "When you see that someone is doing something evil, hate not him, but the devil, who is behind him."

You need to learn to separate the person from the sin he commits. Priests very often observe during Confession that sin is really separate from the person who repents of it. We should be able to turn away from the sinful image of man and remember that everyone, including our enemies and those that hate us, is created according to God's image; and it is this image of God, these rudiments of good that are in everyone, that we should scrutinize.

Why is it necessary to pray for enemies? It is necessary not only for them, but for us as well. We should find in ourselves the strength to be reconciled with people. Archimandrite Sophrony, in his book about St Silouan the Athonite, says: "Those that hate and reject their brother are flawed in their being; they cannot find the way to God, who loves all." This holds true. When hatred for man settles in our heart, we are not able to approach God. As long as we hold on to this feeling, the path to God is barred to us. This is why it is necessary to pray for our enemies.

Every time we approach the Living God, we should be at absolute peace with everyone whom we perceive as our enemies. Let us remember what the Lord said: "Therefore, if you are offering your gift at the altar, and there remember that your brother has something against you, leave your gift there before the altar and go; first be reconciled to your brother, and then come and offer your gift" (Mt 5.23-24). And also other words of the Lord: "Make friends quickly with your accuser while you are in the way with him" (Mt 5.25). "In the way with him" means "in this earthly life." For if we do not manage to be reconciled here with those that hate and offend us, with our enemies, then we will be unreconciled in the future life. And to make up there for what is missing here will no longer be possible.

14

Family Prayer

Up to this point we have spoken primarily about personal, individual prayer. Now I would like to say a few words about prayer in the family circle.

The majority of our contemporaries live in such a way that family members gather fairly rarely, at best twice a day: in the morning for breakfast and in the evening for dinner. During the day, parents are at work, children at school, and only preschoolers and pensioners remain at home. It is very important that, in the daily routine, there be some moments when everyone can gather together for prayer. If a family gathers for dinner, then why not pray for a few minutes together beforehand? You can also read prayers and a selection from the Gospel afterwards.

Common prayer strengthens the family, because family life can only be truly full and happy when its members are joined not only by family ties, but also by spiritual kinship and a common understanding and outlook. Common prayer, moreover, has beneficial effects on every member of the family, and it is particularly helpful for children.

In Soviet times it was forbidden to raise children in a religious spirit. This was motivated by the fact that children were to grow up first, and only later to make an independent choice about whether to go the religious way. There was a deep lie within this argument, because before you can have the opportunity to choose, you must have learned something. And the best age for learning is, of course, childhood. It is very difficult for someone who has learned to live without prayer from childhood to learn to pray. Someone who has been raised from childhood in a prayerful, blessed spirit, who from his earliest years knows about the existence of God and how he can always turn to God, even if he later departs from the Church, will still preserve somewhere in the deep recesses of his soul the skills of prayer and the religious charge obtained in childhood. It often happens that people who have departed from the Church return to God at some stage in their life because in childhood they had become accustomed to prayer.

There is another point. Today in many families there are relatives of the older generation, grandmothers and grandfathers, who were raised in a non-religious environment. Even twenty or thirty years ago you could say that the Church was a place for "grandmas." Now it is grandmothers who represent the most irreligious generation, because they were brought up in the thirties and forties, in the era of "militant atheism." It is very important that older people find their way to church. It is never too late for someone to turn to God, but those young people who already know this path should tactfully, gradually, but consistently engage their older relatives in the orbit of the spiritual life. This can be done particularly well through daily family prayer.

15

Church Prayer

As the renowned twentieth-century theologian Archpriest Georges Florovsky put it, a Christian never prays in solitude: even if he turns to God in his room, closing his door behind him, he still prays as a member of the church community. We are not isolated individuals; we are members of the Church, members of a single body. And we are saved not in isolation, but along with others, with our brothers and sisters. Therefore it is very important that everyone be experienced not only in individual prayer, but also in church prayer, along with other people.

Church prayer has a special significance and meaning. Many of us know by experience how difficult it can be to immerse ourselves in the lines of prayer when alone. But when we come to church, we are immersed in the common prayer of many people, and this prayer takes us into certain depths, and our prayer merges with that of others.

Human life is akin to swimming through a sea or ocean. There are, of course, brave souls who, over-coming storms and tempests, cross the sea alone on a yacht. But, as a rule, people who cross the ocean come together on a ship moving from one bank to another. The Church is this ship in which Christians are moving together along to the path to salvation. And common prayer is one of the most powerful means for advancing on this path.

Much in church, and above all the divine services, encourage prayer. The texts of the divine services used by the Orthodox Church are unusually rich in content; great wisdom is hidden in them. But there is an obstacle faced by many who come to the Church [in Russia]: Church Slavonic. There is much debate today about whether to keep Slavonic in the divine services or to move to Russian. It seems to me that if our divine services were wholly translated into Russian, that a great deal would be lost. Church Slavonic possesses great power, and experience shows that it is not so difficult, that it is not so very different from Russian. One simply needs to expend some effort, such as one would to learn a language or a science, such as mathematics or physics.

Thus, to learn to pray in church, you need to make some effort to go to church more often, perhaps, and to buy the basic divine service books and, in your free time, to study them. Then all the riches of the liturgical language and of the texts of the divine services will unfold before you, and you will see that the divine services are a whole school that teaches you not only prayer, but also the spiritual life.

16

Why Do We Need to Go to Church?

Many people who rarely attend church have a kind of consumer's attitude towards church. They come to church, for instance, before a long trip—to light a candle just for the sake of it, so that nothing will happen on the road. They come for two or three minutes, hurriedly cross themselves and, having lit a candle, go on their way. Some, entering a church, say: "I want to pay money so that Batiushka would pray for such-and-such"—and pay money and leave. The priest needs to pray, but these people themselves do not participate in the prayer.

This is a wrong attitude. The Church is not a candy machine: drop your coin and candy falls out. The Church is a place to go to live and study. If you are experiencing certain difficulties or if one of your neighbors has fallen ill, do not limit yourself to going and lighting a candle. Come to church for the divine service, immerse yourself in prayer, and offer up your needs in prayer along with the priest and the community.

It is important that attendance at church be regular. It is good to attend church every Sunday. The Sunday Divine Liturgy, as well as the Liturgy on great feasts, is the time when we can, by giving up two hours of our earthly affairs, immerse ourselves in the elements of prayer. It is good to come to church with your entire family for Confession and Communion.

If you learn to live from Sunday to Sunday, in the rhythm of the church services, in the rhythm of the Divine Liturgy, then your whole life will change dramatically. Above all, it will become disciplined. The believer knows that next Sunday he will have to give an answer to God, and he lives differently: he does not allow himself many sins that he would otherwise allow himself if he did not go to church. Moreover, the Divine Liturgy itself is an opportunity to receive Holy Communion, that is, to unite with God, not only spiritually, but also physically. Finally, the Divine

Liturgy is a comprehensive service at which the entire church community and each of its members can pray for everyone that troubles or worries him or her. The faithful during the Liturgy can pray for themselves, and for their neighbors, and for their future, bringing repentance for their sins and asking God's blessing for their further ministry. It is very important to learn to participate fully in the Liturgy. In Church there are also other services, for example, the All-Night Vigil—a preparatory service for Communion. You can request supplicatory services for the health of one person or another. But no so-called "private" services—that is, services requested for someone's specific needs—can take the place of the Divine Liturgy, because the Liturgy is the center of church prayer, and it should become the center of the spiritual life of every Christian and every Christian family.

17

On Compunction and Tears

I would like to say a few words about the spiritual and emotional condition that people experience in prayer. Let us recall these verses of Lermontov:

Prayer

In a trying minute of life
If sadness o'erfills the heart,
One miraculous invocation
By rote, without cease I recite.

There is a beneficent will
In the music of living words,
And there breathes in them
An unknown, sacred delight.

> And the soul will release its burden,
> Doubt is far away
> And it's easy to trust, and to cry,
> And I feel so light, so light...

In these beautiful, simple words, the great poet describes what happens to many people during prayer. A person recites the words of prayer, perhaps familiar from childhood, and suddenly he feels a kind of enlightenment, a lightening, and tears. In church language this condition is called *compunction*. It is a condition that is sometimes given during prayer, when a person feels the presence of God more than usual. It is a spiritual state, when the grace of God touches the heart directly.

In the passage from Ivan Bunin's autobiographical book, *The Life of Arseniev*, he describes his teenage years and how, while still a schoolboy, he attended divine services in the parish church of the Exaltation of the Cross. He describes the beginning of the All-Night Vigil, in the shadows of the church, where there are very few people:

> How it all moves me! I am still a boy, an adolescent, but then, I was born endowed with the sense of

all this, and during the past years I have so many times passed through that expectation, that tense silence preceding the service, so many times heard those exclamations and the "amen" that unfailingly follows them and drowns them out, divining beforehand every word of the service, now gives a double response to everything, intensified by its expectation. "Glory to the Holy and Consubstantial..." I hear the pleasant familiar voice coming faintly from the altar, and for the rest of the service I stand as if enchanted. "O come, let us worship God our King! O Come let us worship..." "Bless the Lord, O my soul," I hear, while the priest, preceded by the deacon with a taper, quietly walks about the church, silently filling it with whiffs of the fragrance of incense, and bowing to the icons; and tears dim my eyes, for already I know with certainty that there is, and can be, nothing more beautiful or loftier on earth than all this. And on and on flows the holy mystery. The royal doors are closed and opened alternately, symbolizing now our ejection from the paradise lost by us, now the new contemplation of it; wonderful prayers of light are recited, giving voice to our sorrowful awareness of our earthly weakness, our helplessness, and our eagerness to be led along the path of God.

And Bunin writes that he was able to visit many Western churches where there were organs, that he went into Gothic cathedrals, but he "never wept in those cathedrals as I did in the tiny church of the Exaltation of the Cross on those dark lonely evenings."

It's not just great poets and writers who can describe the grace-filled effects that visiting a church is necessarily bound up with. Everyone can experience it. It is very important that our soul be open to such feelings, so that, coming into church, we be ready to receive the grace of God to the extent to which it is given to us. If a grace-filled state does not come to us and we are not overcome by compunction, we should not worry. This means that our soul is not ripe for compunction. But minutes of such enlightenment are a sign that our prayer is not barren. They testify to the fact that God responds to our prayers and that the grace of God touches our hearts.

18

The Battle with Extraneous Thoughts

One of the main obstacles to attentive prayer is the appearance of extraneous thoughts. St John of Kronstadt, the great ascetic of the end of the nineteenth and beginning of the twentieth centuries, describes in his diaries how, during the celebration of the Divine Liturgy, at the most crucial and sacred moments, before his mind's eye would appear an apple pie or some other reward that he might be given. And with bitter regret he suggests how such extraneous images and thoughts can destroy a prayerful state. If such things happened with the saints, then there is nothing surprising if it happens to us, too. To protect ourselves from extraneous thoughts and images, we have to learn, as did the ancient Fathers of the Church, "to guard our minds."

In the ascetic writers of the Ancient Church there was a detailed development of how outside thoughts gradually penetrate a person. The first stage of this process is called an "article," that is, the sudden appearance of a thought. This thought is still completely alien, but appears somewhere on the horizon; its penetration inside us begins when we begin to pay attention to it, enter into conversation with it, examine and analyze it. Then begins what the Church Fathers call "combination," when man's mind as it were merges with the thought. Finally, the thought turns into a passion and embraces the whole person, and then both prayer and the spiritual life are forgotten.

For this not to happen, it is very important to cut off extraneous thoughts at their first appearance, not allowing them to penetrate deeply into the soul, heart, and mind. Learning to do this requires a lot of work. You cannot but be distracted at prayer, if you do not learn to fight with extraneous thoughts.

One of the diseases of modern man is that he is unable to control the work of his own brain. His brain is autonomous, and thoughts come and go spontaneously. Modern man as a rule does not follow what is going on in his mind. But to learn true prayer, you need to follow your thoughts and to expel ruthlessly those that do not correspond to a prayerful disposition. Short prayers help in overcoming distractions and extraneous thoughts: "Lord, have mercy," "God, be merciful to me, a sinner," and others, which do not require a special focus on the words, but incline one to the birth of feelings and the movement of the heart. With the help of such prayers, you can learn to pray attentively and to focus on prayer.

19

The Jesus Prayer

The Apostle Paul says: Pray without ceasing (1 Thess 5.17). People often ask: How can we pray without ceasing, if we are working, reading, speaking, eating, sleeping, etc? That is, if we are doing things that would seem to be incompatible with prayer? The answer to this question in the Orthodox tradition is the Jesus Prayer. The faithful who practice the Jesus Prayer attain to constant prayer, that is, to a ceaseless standing before God. How is this done?

The Jesus Prayer is: "Lord Jesus Christ, Son of God, have mercy on me, a sinner." There is also a shorter form: "Lord Jesus Christ, have mercy on me." But you can also reduce the prayer to three words: "Lord, have mercy." A person who practices the Jesus Prayer repeats it not only during the divine services or when praying at home, but when travelling, eating, and going to sleep. Even if he is talking with someone or listening to someone, even then, without losing the intensity of his perception, he can nevertheless continue to repeat this prayer in the depths of his heart.

The meaning of the Jesus Prayer does not of course consist in its mechanical repetition, but in always feeling the living presence of Christ. This presence is felt by us first of all because, by pronouncing the Jesus Prayer, we pronounce the name of the Savior.

The name is a symbol of its bearer; in the name is present, as it were, the person to whom it belongs. When a young man falls in love with a young woman, he ceaselessly repeats her name, because she is, as it were, present in her name. And inasmuch as love fills his whole being, he feels the need to repeat this name over and over again. In just the same way, a Christian who loves the Lord repeats the name of Jesus Christ, because his whole heart and being are drawn to Christ.

It is very important when performing the Jesus Prayer not to try to imagine Christ, depicting him like someone in some life situation or, for example, hanging on the Cross. The Jesus Prayer should not be paired with images that might arise in our imagination, because then there is a substitution of real imagination. The Jesus Prayer should be accompanied only by an inner sense of Christ's presence and a feeling of standing before the Living God. No external images are appropriate here.

20

What's So Good About The Jesus Prayer?

The Jesus Prayer has several special properties. First of all, it contains the presence of the name of God.

We often invoke the name of God as if by habit, unthinkingly. We say: "Lord, how tired I am" or "God is with him, let him come another time"—completely not thinking about the force that the name of God possesses. Meanwhile, already in the Old Testament it was commanded: "You shall not take the name of the Lord your God in vain" (Ex 20.7). The ancient Jews related to the name of God with the utmost reverence. In the era following the liberation from the Babylonian captivity, it was generally forbidden to pronounce the name of God. This right was reserved to the high priest alone, once a year, when he entered the Holy of Holies, the main sanctuary of the temple. When we turn with the Jesus Prayer to Christ, our pronunciation of the name of Christ and the confession of him as the Son of God has a completely different significance. This name should be pronounced with the greatest of reverence.

Another property of the Jesus Prayer is its simplicity and accessibility. For reciting the Jesus Prayer, you do not need any specialized books, nor a special place or time. This is its great advantage over many other prayers.

Finally, there is one more property distinguishing this prayer: in it we confess our sins: "Have mercy on me, a sinner." This point is very important, because many of our contemporaries absolutely do not feel their sinfulness. Even at Confession, one frequently hears: "I don't know what to repent of: I live like everyone else; I don't kill or steal," and so on. Meanwhile, it is our sins, as a rule, that are the causes of our major ills and sorrows. A person who is far from God will not recnogize his sins, just as in a dark room we do not see either dust or dirt; but when we open a window, we discover that the room has long needed cleaning.

The soul of man, far from God, is like a dark room. But the nearer you come to God, the more light comes into your soul, and the more sharply you feel your own sinfulness. And this happens not because you compare yourself with other people, but because you stand before God. When we say: "Lord Jesus Christ, have mercy on me, a sinner," we place ourselves before the face of Christ, as it were, comparing our life with his life. And then we will indeed feel ourselves to be sinners and can offer repentance from the depth of our hearts.

21

The Practice of The Jesus Prayer

Let's talk about the practical aspects of the Jesus Prayer. Some people set themselves the task of repeating the Jesus Prayer over the course of the day, say, one hundred, five hundred, or one thousand times. To count how many times they have said the prayer, they use a prayer rope, which may have fifty, one hundred, or more knots. Pronouncing the prayer in their mind, people use a prayer rope. But if you are just beginning the ascetic struggle of the Jesus Prayer, then you should pay more attention to quality, rather than quantity. It seems to me that a person should begin with a very slow pronunciation out loud of the words of the Jesus Prayer, ensuring that the heart participates in the prayer. You pronounce: "Lord... Jesus... Christ... "—and your heart should, like a tuning fork, respond to every word. And do not seek immediately to say the Jesus Prayer many times. Just say it ten times, but if your heart responds to the words of the prayer, that will be enough.

Man has two spiritual centers: the mind and the heart. With the mind are connected intellectual activity, the imagination, and thoughts; with the heart are connected emotions, and experiences. When saying the Jesus Prayer, the center should be the heart. That is why, praying, you should not try to represent anything in the mind—for example, Jesus Christ—but should try to keep your attention in the heart.

The ancient ecclesial ascetic writers developed a technique of "guarding the mind in the heart," whereby the Jesus Prayer was connected with the breathing: when you inhaled, you said "Lord Jesus Christ, Son of God"; and when you exhaled: "have mercy on me, a sinner." A person's attention was, as it were, naturally transferred from the head to the heart. I do not think that everyone should practice the Jesus Prayer in this way; it is enough to say the words of the prayer with great attention and reverence.

Start your morning with the Jesus Prayer. If during the day you have a free minute, recite the prayer a few more times; in the evening, before sleep, repeat it until you fall asleep. If you learn to wake up and fall asleep with the Jesus Prayer, this will give you enormous spiritual support. Gradually, to the extent that your heart becomes more responsive to the words of this prayer, you can reach the point that it becomes unceasing—moreover, the main content of the prayer will not be in pronouncing the words, but in the constant feeling of God's presence in your heart. And if you began by saying the prayer out loud, you will gradually reach the point that you will say it only in your heart, without the involvement of the tongue or lips. You will see how the prayer will transform your entire human nature and all your life. This is the special power of the Jesus Prayer.

22

Books on The Jesus Prayer

"Whatever you do, whatever you happen to be doing at any given time, day and night, pronounce with your mouth these Divine words: 'Lord Jesus Christ, Son of God, have mercy on me, the sinner.' This is not difficult: both while travelling, on the road, and during work—whether you are cutting firewood or carrying water, digging the earth or cooking food. After all, in all these things only the body is at work, and the mind is without occupation—so give it something to do that is inherent and pleasant to its immaterial nature: pronouncing the name of God." This is an excerpt from the book *In the Mountains of the Caucasus*, which was first published in the beginning of the twentieth century and is dedicated to the Jesus Prayer.

I would like to emphasize that this prayer needs to be learned—moreover, preferably with the help of a spiritual director. In the Orthodox Church there are teachers of prayer among monastics, pastors, and even the laity: these are people who have themselves learned the power of prayer by experience. But if you do not find such an instructor—and many complain that it is now hard to find instructors in prayer—you can turn to books such as *In the Mountains of the Caucasus* or *The Way of a Pilgrim*.

The latter, which was published in the nineteenth century and reprinted many times, is about a person who decided to learn unceasing prayer. He was a wanderer who walked from city to city with a bag on his shoulders and a staff, who learned to pray. He repeated the Jesus Prayer several thousand times a day.

There is also the classic five-volume collection of the works of the Holy Fathers from the fourth to the fourteenth century: *The Philokalia*. This is a very rich treasury of spiritual experience, containing many instructions about the Jesus Prayer and sobriety or mental vigilance. Those who truly desire to learn how to pray should become acquainted with these books.

I also quoted a passage from the book *In the Mountains of the Caucasus* because many years ago, when I was an adolescent, I had the opportunity to travel to Georgia, to the Caucasus Mountains near Sukhumi. There I met hermits. They lived there even in Soviet times, away from worldly vanity, in caves, gorges, and precipices, and no one knew of their existence. They lived by prayer and passed on a treasury of prayerful experience from generation to generation. These were people who were as if from a different world, who had attained great spiritual heights and profound inner peace. And it was all thanks to the Jesus Prayer.

May God grant that, through experienced instructors and through the books of the Holy Fathers, that we learn this treasure: the unceasing practice of the Jesus Prayer!

23

"Our Father, Who Art in Heaven"

The "Our Father" is of special significance, because Jesus Christ himself gave it to us. It begins with the words: "Our Father, who art in heaven." This prayer is comprehensive in character: in it is concentrated, as it were, everything that man needs both for earthly life and for the salvation of his soul. The Lord gave it to us so that we would know what we should pray for and what to ask of God.

The first words of this prayer, "Our Father, who art in heaven," reveal to us that God is not some distant or abstract being, not some notional good foundation, but our Father. Today very many people, in response to the question of whether they believe in God, reply in the affirmative; but if you ask them how they imagine God and what they think of him, they respond something like this: "Well, God is good, it is something luminous, some kind of positive energy." That is, they treat God like some kind of abstraction, as something impersonal.

When we begin our prayer with the words "Our Father," then we are immediately appealing to the personal, living God, to God as Father—to the Father about whom Christ spoke in the parable of the prodigal son. Many people remember the subject of this parable from the Gospel according to Luke. The son decided to leave his father, not waiting for his death. He received the inheritance due to him, went to a far country, and there squandered his inheritance. When he had reached the final limit of poverty and exhaustion, he decided to return to his father. He said to himself: I will arise and go to my father, and will say unto him, Father, I have sinned against heaven, and before you, and am no longer worthy to be called your son: make me as one of your hired servants (Lk 15.18-19). And when he was still far off, his father ran to meet him, throwing himself on his neck. The son was not even able to say his prepared words, because the father immediately gave him a ring, the sign of filial dignity, and clothed him in his former clothes—that is, he completely restored him to a son's dignity. This is precisely the way God treats us. We are not hirelings, but sons of God, and the Lord treats us like his children. Therefore our attitude towards God should be characterized by devotion and noble, filial love.

When we pronounce "Our Father," this means that we are not praying in isolation, as individuals, each one of which has his own father, but as members of a single human family, a single Church, a single Body of Christ. In other words, by calling God our father, we imply that all other people are our brethren. Moreover, when Christ teaches us in prayer to turn to God as "Our Father," he places himself as it were on the same level with us. St Symeon the New Theologian said that through faith in Christ we become Christ's brethren, because we share with him a common father: our heavenly Father.

As for the words, "who art in heaven," they do not indicate the physical heavens, but that God lives in a completely different dimension from us, that he is absolutely transcendent to us. But through prayer, through the Church, we have the opportunity to join in this other world.

24

"Hallowed Be Thy Name"

What do the words "Hallowed be thy Name" mean? The Name of God is already holy in itself, bearing within it itself the force of holiness, spiritual strength, and the presence of God. Why do we need to pray in these words? Could it really be that the Name of God won't remain holy if we don't say "Hallowed be thy Name"?

When we say "Hallowed be thy Name," we primarily have in mind that the Name of God should be hallowed, that is, be revealed as holy through us, Christians, through our spiritual life. The apostle Paul, addressing the unworthy Christians of his time, said: "For, as it is written, 'the name of God is blasphemed among the Gentiles because of you'" (Rom

2.24; Is 52.5). These are very important words. They speak of our discrepancy with the spiritual-moral norm that is contained in the Gospel and according to which we, Christians, are obliged to live. This discrepancy is, perhaps, one of the main tragedies both for us as Christians and for the entire Christian Church.

The Church possesses holiness, because it is built on the Name of God, which itself is holy. Members of the Church are far from consistent with the norms that the Church advances. One often hears reproaches— and rightly so—addressed to Christians: "How can you prove the existence of God, if you yourself live no better—and sometimes even worse—than pagans and atheists? How do you reconcile faith in God with unworthy actions?" Thus, each one of us should ask ourselves daily: "Do I correspond as a Christian to the ideal of the Gospel? Is the Name of God hallowed or blasphemed by me? Am I an example of a true Christian, who has love, humility, meekness, and mercy? Or am I an example of the opposite of these virtues?"

Often people turn to priests with the question: "What should I do to bring my son (daughter, husband, mother, father) to church? I talk to them about God, but they don't want to listen." The problem is that it isn't enough just to talk about God. When someone who has become a believer tries to convert others to his faith, especially those close to him, with the help of words, persuasion, and sometimes even coercion, urging them to pray or go to church, this often leads to the opposite result: his neighbors reject everything ecclesial and spiritual. We can bring people to the Church only when we ourselves become true Christians; when they, looking at us, can say: "Yes, now I understand what Christian faith can do for someone, how it can change and transform him; I will begin to believe in God, because I see how Christians differ from non-Christians."

25

"Thy Kingdom Come"

What do these words mean? After all, the Kingdom of God will inevitably come, the world will end, and mankind will enter into another dimension. Obviously, we are not praying for the end of the world, but that the Kingdom of God come to us, that is, that it would become real in our lives, that our present—humdrum, gray, and sometimes dark and tragic—earthly lives would be permeated by the presence of the Kingdom of God.

What is the Kingdom of God? In order to reply to this question, we need to turn to the Gospel and remember that Jesus Christ began his preaching with the words: "Repent: for the kingdom of heaven is at hand" (Mt 4.17). Then Christ repeatedly spoke to people of his Kingdom; he did not object when he was called a King—for instance, when he entered Jerusalem and was greeted as the King of the Jews. Even when on trial and being mocked, slandered, and maligned, the Lord replied to Pilate's apparently ironic question—Are you the King of the Jews?—with the words: "My kingdom is not of this world" (Mt 18.33-36). These words of the Savior also contain an answer to the question of what the Kingdom of God is. When we turn to God with the words "Thy Kingdom come," we are asking that this otherworldly and spiritual Kingdom of Christ become a reality in our lives, that the spiritual dimension about which so many speak, but which so few know by experience, would become manifest in our lives.

When the Lord Jesus Christ told his disciples what awaited him in Jerusalem—torments, suffering, and death on the Cross—the mother of two of them said to him: "Grant that these two sons of mine may sit, one at your right hand and one at your left, in your kingdom" (Mt 20.21). He was speaking of how he must suffer and die, but she imagined a Man on a royal throne and wanted her sons to be next to him. But, as we understand, the Kingdom of God was first revealed on the Cross: Christ was crucified, bleeding profusely, and above him hung a sign: "King of the Jews." It was only later that the Kingdom of God was revealed in the glorious and saving Resurrection of Christ. It was this Kingdom that we were promised: a Kingdom that is given through great efforts and tribulations. The path to the Kingdom of God lies through Gethsemane and Golgotha: through the trials, temptations, sorrows, and sufferings that befall all of us. We should remember this when we say the prayer "Thy Kingdom come."

26

"Thy Will Be Done, On Earth as it Is in Heaven"

How lightly we speak these words! And how very rarely do we recognize that our will might not coincide with God's will. After all, sometimes God sends us suffering, but we turn out to be incapable of accepting it as sent by God, and we murmur indignantly. How often do people, coming up to a priest, say: "I cannot agree with such-and-such; I understand that it's God's will, but I cannot come to terms with it." What can you say to such a person? It's not as if you can tell him that, when saying the Lord's Prayer, he needs to replace the words "Thy will be done" with "My will be done"!

Each of us needs to struggle so that our will may correspond with God's good will. We say: "Thy will be done, on earth as it is in Heaven." That is, God's will, which is already accomplished in Heaven, in the spiritual world, should also be accomplished here, on earth—and above all in our own lives. And we should be ready to follow God's voice in everything. We need to find the strength within ourselves to deny our own will for the sake of fulfilling God's will. Often, when praying, we ask for something from God, but we do not receive it. And then it seems to us that our prayer has not been heard. We need to find the strength within ourselves to accept this "refusal" on God's part as his will.

Recall Christ, who, on the eve of his death, prayed to his Father, saying: "O my father, if it be possible, let this cup pass from me." But the cup did not pass, which means that the answer to his prayer was different: Jesus Christ was to drink this cup of suffering, affliction, and death. Knowing this, he said to the Father: "nevertheless, not as I will, but as thou wilt" (Mt 26.39-42).

Such should be our relationship to God's will, too. If we feel that some affliction is coming our way and that we will have to drink from a cup for which we might not have the strength, we can say: "Lord, if it is possible, take this cup of sorrow from me, let is pass from me." But, like Christ, we should conclude our prayer with the words: "But not my will, but thine be done."

We need to relate to God with confidence. Children often ask their parents for something that the latter don't give them because they consider it to be dangerous. Years go by, and we understand just how right our parents were. So it is with us. Time passes, and we suddenly understand just how much more beneficial what the Lord sent us was than what we had wanted to get according to our own will.

27

"Give Us This Day Our Daily Bread"

We can turn to God with a great variety of petitions. We can ask him not only for that which is sublime and spiritual, but also for that which is essential for us on the material plane. "Daily bread" is what we live on; it's our daily nourishment. Moreover, in the prayer we say: "Give us this day our daily bread." In other words, we don't ask God to provide us with everything necessary for all the subsequent days of our lives. We ask him for daily food, knowing that if he feeds us today, then he will feed us tomorrow, too. Pronouncing these words, we express our trust in God: we trust him with our life today, just as we trust him for tomorrow.

The words "daily bread" indicate that which is necessary for life, and not anything excessive. A person might set out on the way of acquisitiveness and, having everything necessary—a roof over his head, a piece of bread, and a minimum of material goods—begin to engage in hoarding and luxury. That way leads to a dead end, because the more he accumulates and the more money he has, the more he feels the emptiness of life, feeling that there are other needs that cannot be satisfied with material goods. Thus, "daily bread" is that which is essential. It is not a limousine, nor palaces, nor millions of dollars—it is that without which neither we, nor our children, nor our kinsmen can live.

Some understand the words "daily bread" in a more elevated sense: as "super-essential." In particular, the Greek Church Fathers wrote that "super-essential bread" is the Bread that comes down from heaven—in other words, Christ himself, whom Christians receive in the Mystery of Holy Communion. Such an understanding is also justifiable, because, besides material bread, we also need spiritual bread.

Everyone can invest his own content into the concept of "daily bread." During the war, a boy prayed:

"Give us this day our daily bread," because his main food was dried bread. The main thing necessary for the boy and his family for sustaining life was dried bread. This might seem funny or sad, but it shows that everyone—both old and young—asks God for what he needs most of all, for that without which he cannot live for a single day.

28

"And Forgive Us Our Trespasses, As We Forgive Those Who Trespass Against Us"

Prayer is inextricably bound up with a person's way of life. The reason for the difficulties a person experiences in prayer lies in an incorrect, unspiritual, and non-evangelical life. We sense this especially when we say the "Our Father." Each petition of this prayer places us in front of a given reality, as if we were being judged—judged by our own conscience. And this prayer, if we pray from our soul and heart—if we really think about what is written here—should constantly force us to change our lives.

We say: "And forgive us our trespasses, as we forgive those who trespass against us," that is, we ask God to forgive us our debts, as we forgive those who are in debt to us. When we speak these words, we should ask ourselves: do we forgive our neighbors? Are we ready to place our own forgiveness by God in dependence on whether we forgive others? Isn't this too frightening? Isn't this too much responsibility?

Experience shows that it isn't so difficult to forgive everyone, just as it isn't so difficult to love everyone—everyone, in an abstract sense. Many people say: I love people, I just can't come to terms with two or three people—my neighbors, my co-workers, my mother in law—but I love everyone else. Thus, the words "forgive us our trespasses, as we forgive those who trespass against us" reminds us of the couple of people that we can't forgive, whose debts we can't forgive. And this prayer teaches us that, as long as we don't forgive them, we can't hope that the Lord will forgive us.

Earthly life is given to us so that we might make peace with everyone. In life many knots are tied, and it is our task to manage to untie them while we still have time. Nothing is impossible for man. It can be very difficult to make peace with someone, to forgive someone, but if we don't find the strength for this, we can't count on God to forgive us. If we call God our Father and ourselves Christians, if we say "Hallowed be thy Name"—that is, that the name of God should be holy, and the holiness of God's name should be manifest through our deeds—then how can we not forgive our debtors, those who have offended, insulted, or humiliated us?

Christian life is an ascetic struggle, and we should relate to it responsibly; we should earn the right to say the Lord's Prayer. And we earn this right through our good deeds. No single word—and, moreover, no word of prayer—should be in vain, empty, or unjustified. Behind every word there is a reality, and behind the words of the "Our Father" should stand our actions. If we say to God: "Thy will be done," that means that we should submit our will to his will, to God's will. And if we ask God: "And forgive us our trespasses, as we forgive those who trespass against us," this means that we should learn to forgive everyone we consider blameworthy, whom we consider to be in our debt.

29

"And Lead Us Not into Temptation, but Deliver Us from the Evil One"

What is temptation and who is the evil one?

Temptation is a test that is either sent to us from God, or comes from the devil, but is allowed by God. Every temptation for us is a kind of endurance test. And sometimes we pass this test, and sometimes we don't. When we ask God: "And lead us not into temptation," we are as it were saying to God: "Do not send us a test beyond our strength; send us the kind that we can deal with, so that the trials and tribulations that You send will not crush us or kill our faith."

The evil one is the devil, the enemy of the human race. With regard to the devil, we must avoid two extremes. Some tend to deny the existence of the devil and demons. These people—believers or unbelievers—do not recognize the real existence in this world of evil powers; moreover, not as abstract powers, but as living beings, because the devil and demons, like angels, are real, living beings. There is another extreme, especially widespread among believing and churchly people who exaggerate the importance of the devil, who become so afraid of the actions of the devil and evil powers, that they live in a semi-paralyzed condition. Hence the common fear among believers of the evil eye, black magic, and the like. A timid approach to life can also come from this fear, when a person scared of everything, when he sees threats everywhere can't live creatively, freely, or fully.

We should remember that evil, of course, has power and can have a negative, even devastating impact on our lives, but only when we ourselves allow it access to us. The devil is powerless where he isn't invited, where his presence isn't wanted. If a person goes to church, prays, wears a cross, and makes the sign of the cross; if he fulfills God's commandments and refrains from sins, then the devil is powerless and has no place in such a person. When does the devil gain strength? When a person opens the floodgates and vents in his home; when, for instance, he falls into a given passion, such as an addiction to drugs or alcohol. The danger of alcoholism is not that people drink more wine than they should; it's that it weakens them and opens the way for the devil to get inside their souls.

Therefore, when we pray to God: "Deliver us from the evil one," we are asking that he would always grant us the power to refrain from that which gives the evil one power over our lives. And if we learn this, then neither the devil, nor any other dark power, nor black magic, nor anything like it can have any effect on us.

30

Prayer to the Mother of God

Orthodox Christians pray not only to God, but also to the Mother of God and the saints. This practice of prayer in the Orthodox Church differs, for example, from the practice of Protestant communities. Protestants do not recognize prayer to the Mother of God and the saints. They say: we do not need intermediaries to approach God. This is a fair remark—we do not need "intermediaries"—but the conclusion drawn therefrom is wrong. After all, we don't pray to the Mother of God as to a kind of middle tier between us and God; we pray to her because she is the Mother of God, because it is impossible to separate her from her Divine Son.

When I was studying in England, my professor—an elderly Orthodox bishop—often invited me for studies in his home. I would go to his house, and his elderly mother would open the door for me. Imagine if I didn't greet her, if I didn't notice her, but passed right by her into the house saying: "I don't need any intermediaries; I only deal with the bishop." It seemed to me perfectly natural that, dealing with the son, I also dealt with the mother. Of course, this argument is of a purely everyday character.

There are also more serious arguments. The most important of these is the experience of millions of people who show that the Mother of God listens to their prayers and replies to them; that she helps people; and, moreover, that she is indeed an intercessor for people before her Son and God.

The Mother of God is inseparable from the Savior; her undertaking is inseparable from his. Consider that when the Angel of the Lord descended from heaven to say to her: "you will conceive in your womb and bear a son" (Lk 1.31), the Incarnation depended upon her agreement or disagreement. She could have said "no," but she said "yes." She raised the Child, brought him to the Temple in sacrifice to God; She traversed his entire earthly life alongside him. When Christ was crucified, she stood at the Cross, because she could not be separated from him. She was with him even in his most fearful suffering, because she became a participant in his exploit.

When the Lord was on the Cross, his beloved disciple stood next to him, and he said to her: "'Woman, behold your son!' Then he said to his disciple, 'Behold your mother!'" (Jn 19.26-27). He thereby, as it were, gave over not only to his beloved disciple, but to all his disciples, her protection and care. From that moment she, as the Mother of her Son, also became the Mother of his followers, that is, the Mother of the Church. And we turn to her as to our Mother and the Mother of the Church.

We say in prayer to the Mother of God: "Most Holy Theotokos, save us." This doesn't mean that we consider her to be our savior. The Savior is Christ. But we confess her involvement in the mystery of salvation, her participation in this mystery. And we understand that salvation is possible for us because the Mother of God expressed her agreement with the word of God addressed to her. And, thanks to her consent, we have access to her Son and her God, our heavenly Father.

31

Prayer to the Saints

The tradition of the veneration of saints in the Christian Church is very ancient; it has existed from the very moment of the Church's appearance, from the first years of its existence. Christian churches in antiquity were built on the graves of martyrs. And it was the blood of martyrs, according to the words of one ancient ecclesial writer, that was the "seed of Christianity"; that is, Christianity spread through the sacrifice of the martyrs.

The martyrs are people who showed by the example of their own life and death that man can repeat Christ's sacrifice; that earthly man, for all his weaknesses and infirmities, can likewise sacrifice himself for people and for God, as did Jesus Christ. He who offered himself in sacrifice became a spiritual hero in the eyes of other people, especially in the eyes of those who knew him. The veneration of this saint began immediately after his death. The tradition has been preserved to the present day according to which an Orthodox church must have at least a small particle of a saint. One should not perform the Divine Liturgy on a simple table: it is to be performed on a Holy Table or special board into which part of the relics of a saint is sewn. The reason for this is that martyrs and saints are the foundation upon which the Christian Church is built. We pray to saints because these were people who, although they were like us, thanks to the exploit of their lives, attained deification, becoming like Christ. We pray to them because they followed the path that we are trying to follow. And the experience of many Christians witnesses to the fact that the saints hear our prayers and answer them.

I'd like to mention very briefly one negative phenomenon connected with the veneration of the saints. The fact is that some people regard the saints rather like the pagans regarded their gods: on the principle of "what saint can help with what." Such people go to church and ask: "To what saint should I light a candle in order to get an apartment?" "To what saint should I pray for a toothache," etc. We should remember that the saints are not some kind of idols from which we can obtain something special. The saints are not specialists in finding apartments, in curing toothaches, or other similar things. There are, of course, saints who were doctors during their lives, and we turn to them with appeals for healing, such as the Holy Great-Martyr Panteleimon. And, indeed, through the prayers of such saints many healings do occur. But by no means should we regard the saints as a sort of fetish: we shouldn't replace prayer to the saints, as to people who attained spiritual perfection and who can help us in prayer, with prayer to the saints as some sort of idols that are needed only for attaining specific help.

The saints are above all our heavenly friends, who can help us progress on the path to salvation, on the path to God. And only secondarily are saints those that can help us in specific, everyday matters.

32

Life Is Impossible without Prayer

To sum up our talk about prayer: prayer is above all a conversation with God, an encounter with him; it's a dialogue that involves not only our own words addressed to God, but also God's answer. Therefore it's important that we be able not only to speak, but also to be silent, so that we can listen to those Divine depths that are revealed to us through prayer.

In prayer we need to be absolutely honest. Here there can't be anything ambiguous or artificial. We need to stand before God as we are and say to him what needs to be said, what we are thinking and feeling. Therefore, for communion with God there's no need to think up a special language, to look for special words, or to choose special topics. We should pray to God for what our heart is asking and yearning for.

We need to pray continuously. It isn't enough to pray from time to time, only when we need something from God; we should be always praying: morning, evening, and over the course of the day and our entire life. And at the center of our prayer shouldn't be anything specific that we're asking for from God, but God himself, because the main content of prayer is always our encounter with God, the possibility of discovering him for ourselves.

We should pray not only for ourselves, but also for others; not only for our relatives and friends, but for our enemies. We should pray to God not as isolated individuals, but as people who represent a portion of humanity, addressing God not only on our own behalf, but also on behalf of one human family, for God is the heavenly Father of each one of us.

We pray not only to God, but also to the Mother of God and the saints because they are our heavenly protectors, our heavenly intercessors. We pray to our Guardian Angel that he would guard us in all our ways.

We pray not only for the living, but also for the departed, that the Lord would grant them peace and repose.

Once again I'd like to emphasize that prayer should be the foundation of our life, that upon which our whole life should be configured. The Christian life should correspond to prayer. If a person is unsuccessful in prayer, it means that he is living wrongly, that his spiritual condition doesn't correspond to prayer.

Let us learn to pray; let us work so that prayer would reach our heart and, through our heart, ascend to the heavenly heights to reach God. Let us work on ourselves, that prayer would become the core and foundation of our life. Let us ask God, the Mother of God, and the saints, that they would teach us to pray, because life without prayer is impossible, just as it's impossible to live and be saved without God and his Church.